j612
S21b

A662603-1

CL

LIFE EDUCATION

Bodyworks

Written by
Pete Sanders & Steve Myers
Illustrated by
Derek Matthews and Paul Banville

FRANKLIN WATTS
A Division of Grolier Publishing
LONDON • NEW YORK • HONG KONG • SYDNEY
DANBURY, CONNECTICUT

First American Edition ©1997 by
Franklin Watts
A Division of Grolier Publishing
Sherman Turnpike
Danbury, CT 06816

Sanders, Pete.
    Bodyworks / Pete Sanders and Steve Myers.
        p. cm. -- (Life education)
    Includes index.
    Summary: Discusses the various parts of
the human body and how each functions.
    ISBN 0-531-14427-5
    1. Human physiology--Juvenile literature. 2.
Human anatomy--Juvenile literature. [1.
Body, Human. 2. Human physiology. 3.
Human anatomy.] I. Myers, Steve. II. Title.
III. Series.
    QP37.S26 1997
    612--dc20   96-13325
                                       CIP AC

Edited by: Helen Lanz
Designed by: Sally Boothroyd
Commissioned photography by:
Peter Millard
Illustrations by: Derek Matthews
and Paul Banville
Medical consultant: Dr. M. Redfern

Acknowledgments:
Commissioned photography by Peter Millard:
cover; title page.
Researched photography: Bubbles 15 (bottom)
(I. West); Eye Ubiquitous 8 (R. Chester); Franklin
Watts CD transparency; John Walmsley 29; Rex
Features 15 (top) (E. Catarina); Robert Harding 5
(H. Kern), 6; Science Photo Library 9
(S. Camazine), 12, 17 (K. Eward), 20 (H. Young),
22; Zefa 11, 19 (H. Sochurek), 24, 26 (Norman).
Artwork: Cartoon illustrations by Derek
Matthews throughout.
Anatomical illustrations by Paul Banville: 6, 9, 12,
13, 14, 16, 24.

Franklin Watts and Life Education
International are indebted to Susan Kaplin,
Amanda Friend, Vince Hatton, and Laurie
Noffs for their invaluable help.

Franklin Watts would like to extend their
special thanks to all the actors who appear
in the Life Education books (Key Stage 3):

Hester Cann   Chloe Parsons
James Ceppi di Lecco   Dipali Patel
James Chandler

*'Each second we live is a new and unique moment of the universe, a moment that
will never be again...And what do we teach our children? We teach them that two
and two make four and that Paris is the capital of France.*

*When will we also teach them: do you know who you are? You are a marvel. You
are unique. In all the years that have passed, there has never been another child
like you. And look at your body – what a wonder it is! Your legs, your arms, your
clever fingers, the way you move. You may become a Shakespeare, a Michelangelo,
a Beethoven. You have the capacity for anything. Yes, you are a marvel. And
when you grow up, can you then harm another who is, like you, a marvel? You
must cherish one another. You must work – we must all work – to make this world
worthy of its children.'*

Pablo Casals

A famous Spanish musician, also noted for his humanitarian beliefs.

(1876 - 1973)

CONTENTS

Get ready to
use your brains
and expand your
minds. We're going to
look at YOU in the world.

A HEALTHY BALANCE

Congratulations! You are the owner of the most incredibly sophisticated piece of equipment in the world. It is capable of performing tasks that many machines find impossible. It can process and interpret information in ways that even the best computers cannot. It can grow, move around, repair itself – even reproduce. It distinguishes you from other animals by giving you the capacity to speak, feel, and think. It's truly amazing, and it's yours for free. It's your own body!

BIOLOGY LESSON

You use your body all day, but it's sometimes easy to forget just how complex and miraculous it actually is.

Mom, did you know that you don't hear sound? Sound waves enter your ear and cause vibrations. Your brain works out what they are and converts them into what you hear. **Amazing!**

I know sound causes vibrations because that music of yours is making the house shake! Please turn it down, Ben. Otherwise my brain will send a message to the muscles in my legs, causing me to walk over there to turn it off!

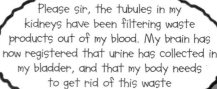

Please sir, the tubules in my kidneys have been filtering waste products out of my blood. My brain has now registered that urine has collected in my bladder, and that my body needs to get rid of this waste product.

He means he needs to go to the bathroom.

Thank you, Franny. In fact Ben's brain registers the need to empty the bladder when it's only about half full. It's only ten minutes until break.

He means you'll have to cross your legs!

Since when have you liked vegetables?

Yes, Ben. Last time we gave you sprouts you said we were trying to poison you.

That was before I found out how good they are for you. They're full of nutrients, which is what my body needs to help me play football. Did you know that every single thing you put in your body can have an effect on how well your body works? Incredible, isn't it?

BALANCING ACT

Everything your body does requires balance. You only have to think about the way the body is designed and arranged – two eyes, two ears, two arms, two legs, and so on – to see some of the more obvious examples of this. Others are less apparent. Breathing takes in oxygen to the lungs and releases carbon dioxide. The two gases are exchanged to keep the correct balance of each.

ALL TOGETHER NOW!

Your body is performing its own complicated balancing act every day of your life. It is called homeostasis. This is the process by which all the systems of your body work together to control such things as your temperature, blood pressure, and heart rate, to keep everything working at its best. It is also responsible for recognizing when damaged cells need repairing and when the body needs defending against disease. Decisions you make about your lifestyle affect your homeostasis – what you eat, medicines you may take. It may (or may not) seem unlikely now – but as you get older you might be encouraged to smoke cigarettes, drink alcohol or try other drugs. Your decisions about whether or not you will do this will affect how your body performs for you.

Many choices in life are about achieving a balance. This boy has chosen to train to achieve this balance!

Greg is too cold. His body is trying to balance this by making him shiver. This makes his muscles work, burning nutrients and creating warmth.

Fatima's body is at its normal homeostatic temperature of 98.6° F (38° C).

Jack is too warm. His body has realized this and is producing sweat to cool itself down.

Greg and Jack's bodies are working to try to return them to a state of homeostasis.

What have you done today? How many times were you aware of your body working? How do you think you can help your body maintain its homeostasis?

THE INSIDE STORY

Whenever you look in a mirror you only see a small part of what you really are. What you see on the outside of your body is linked to what is happening on the inside. Although every human body is made and works in basically the same way, there are elements within the body that ensure each of us is different and special. There is nobody else on the planet, even if you have a twin brother or sister, who is exactly like you.

From cell to organ

BODY BUILDERS

All living matter is made up of tiny structures, called cells, which are so small that they can be seen properly only by using a microscope. Every cell in your body has the same basic components – a nucleus which contains all the information the cell needs, cytoplasm, which is like a thick liquid, and a cell membrane, a thin "wall" that encloses each cell. However, not all cells are the same size or shape, nor do they all have the same function.

A cell seen individually, as part of a sheet of tissue and as part of the heart.

> **!** *They are called cells, because Robert Hook, the first person to see these structures thought they looked like minute prison cells!*

Cells are constantly dying off and being replaced. A large proportion of the dust in every home is made of dead skin cells!

GETTING ORGANIZED

Hundreds of cells of a few types grouped together to form tissues. When several different tissues work together to make a structure with a particular function, that structure is called an organ. Organs in your body include the heart, kidneys, liver, lungs, eyes, and the most important one of all – the brain.

A SYSTEMATIC APPROACH

Organs that work together to perform special tasks become a body system. Those in your body are the skeletal system, the muscle system, the respiratory system, the circulatory system, the brain and central nervous system, the immune and lymphatic system, the digestive system, the endocrine system, and the reproductive system.

Question: What is the largest and heaviest organ in your body?

Answer: Your skin! In an adult it can weigh up to 19.8 pounds.

YOU-NIQUE!

All the body systems working together make up an independent organism. In other words, YOU! And don't fall into the trap of thinking that they only make up your actual body and not the whole you. After all, where does one start and the other end? Everything about you – movements, moods, sights and sounds, all your ideas – comes to you thanks to the way in which your body works. That's why it's worth understanding exactly how it works, and what you can do to make sure it keeps on working at its best. You'd have a hard time getting along without it!

LONG DIVISION

The fully grown human body contains more than 50 billion cells. Incredible as it sounds, though, you started life as one single cell. It contained all the information needed to become you as you are today. When you grow, it is not because the cells get bigger, but because they increase in number, by dividing in half again and again. Each newly formed set of two cells is an exact replica of the previous one. Of the new cells, one may go on to divide again and the other may stop dividing and take on a special function.

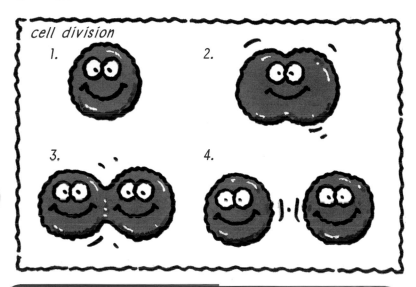

cell division
1.
2.
3.
4.

HOME SWEET CHROMOSOME!

The nucleus of every cell contains 46 chromosomes. These tiny structures hold all the "instructions" that go to make up you.

A DNA strand resembles an incredibly long, twisted ladder and there is a virtually infinite number of ways in which the "rungs" of this ladder can be arranged.

They are made of a substance called DNA. Segments of DNA make up "code chemicals," called genes. Genes determine such things as what sex you are, the color of your eyes, your eventual height, and so on. The action of genes depends on where the cell ends up in the body. A gene for "curly hair" will have no effect in a muscle cell, thank goodness!

SKELETON KEY

What keeps you from slumping to the ground when you stand up? The 206 bones that make up your skeletal system, or skeleton. This is what gives each of us our basic shape. Without it, you'd resemble something like a huge jellyfish! Your bones act as a framework for your muscles, protect many of your organs from damage and give your body flexibility. And as if this isn't enough, some bones are hollow. They contain a jelly-like substance called bone marrow, which makes blood cells.

BRAIN BOX

Your skull is made of 29 bony plates joined together. It is responsible for protecting the main sense organs – the eyes, ears, and nose – and encloses and protects the most important organ of all – your brain.

Your hands and feet contain nearly half the bones in your body. That's why they can perform such intricate tasks. Scientists have been trying for years to create a similarly efficient device, and they haven't succeeded yet!

JOINT VENTURES

The place where two bones meet is called a joint. The bones forming the joint are held in place by tough strings of tissue, known as ligaments.

Some joints are fixed and do not move – such as those in the skull where small plates of bone meet. Others do allow movement, but in particular ways. Your neck forms what is known as a pivot joint.

Your knees and elbows can bend in one direction, but not the other, and they don't bend from side to side. These are called hinge joints.

Your hips and shoulders, on the other hand, can move in all directions. These are known as ball and socket joints.

If you think you've heard these terms before, you probably have. Builders, architects, and engineers use similar ideas in designing many of the things we use every day. Each time you open a door you see an example of a hinge joint – unless it's a revolving door of course!

Everyone is taller in the morning than the evening! It sounds odd, but during the day the weight of your body on your spine gradually squashes the discs of cartilage very slightly. When you lie down to sleep, this pressure is released.

BACK-CHAT

Your spine, or backbone, is made up of small, specially shaped bones, called vertebrae. They are designed to fit one on top of the other, like stacking chairs, separated by discs of cartilage. They form a long hollow tube that encloses the spinal cord. It is this cord that carries most of the messages from the brain to the rest of the body, and vice versa.

MIND YOUR BACK

Damage to your spine can be very painful and serious. Many injuries occur because people don't support their backs when lifting or moving heavy objects. The trick is not to put the strain of the weight on your back itself, but to let the muscles in your arms and legs do the hard work. That's what they're there for, after all.

LAZY BONES

Bones are very strong, but they can be broken. Most broken bones, however, can be mended. To allow this to happen, it is vital that the bone is held in place in one position. This is why anyone who breaks an arm or leg usually has it set in a cast, to prevent movement. It might seem a hassle at the time, but it lets the bone cells get to work in forming new cells that can then "knit" together.

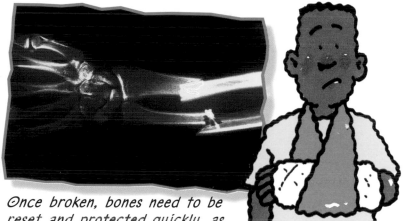

Once broken, bones need to be reset and protected quickly, as they begin to mend immediately.

SHOCK ABSORBER

Cartilage is the body's natural cushion. Where two bones meet, a layer of cartilage and fluid between them stops them from rubbing together, which would both damage them and be very painful. Cartilage is also the substance that forms your nose and ears. It is a strong and very flexible substance.

Taking care of your back can stop aches and pains in other parts of your body, too, and improve your posture.

The right kind of footwear can help to absorb some of the shock of walking or running, which would otherwise be felt by your back. But this doesn't mean you have to buy the latest, most expensive pair of shoes you can find!

MUSCLE BOUND

Your skeleton is strong, flexible, and protective. But it can't move on its own – it needs muscles. You are probably aware of some, such as those in your arms and legs. Your body has almost 700 muscles altogether, and not only do they keep you moving, they keep your heart beating, move food through your body, and allow you to breathe. And you exercise your body's biggest muscle every time you sit down!

TWO'S COMPANY

Muscles often work in pairs to achieve particular movements. A muscle can only become shorter – it can't make itself longer. When you bend your arm, the muscle at the front of your upper arm contracts and the one at the back of the arm relaxes, forcing the forearm upward. When you straighten the arm again, the opposite happens. It's a bit like a seesaw. You have the power to force the board down, but need someone else on the other end to make it rise again!

The biggest muscle in the body is the gluteus maximus — otherwise known as your bottom! You don't just sit on it though. It helps you to walk and run, as well as sit down and stand up again. The longest muscle is the sartorius in your thigh. It's thanks to this muscle that you can cross your legs!

THE FORCE IS WITH YOU!

Some movements also rely on outside factors. To understand this, stand upright and still with your knees straight. Now try to jump in the air without bending your knees or ankles. Unless you've learned the power of levitation, you won't be going anywhere! To achieve height you need to bend your legs and push off from the ground. When you walk, you are not only using the muscles in your legs, you are also pushing your feet against the ground to carry yourself along.

SHAKE A LEG!

Muscles that you can work by making a conscious decision to do so, such as those in your arms and hands, are called voluntary muscles. Many muscles also work without your having to make any effort. For instance, although you can breathe in and out at will, your muscles will continue to make you breathe, whether you are thinking about it or not.

LEAVE IT TO US

Some of your muscles you couldn't consciously influence if you wanted to. They are known as involuntary muscles, because you have no control over them. Their function is so important that your body takes over. Examples are the muscles in your throat, which squeeze food down into the stomach, and the heart, which beats because of regular muscular contractions.

TOO HOT TO HANDLE!

If you accidentally put your hand on a very hot surface, the reaction of your arm will be immediate. The message that you are in danger of burning yourself registers almost instantaneously in your spinal cord, which sends out further messages to the muscles to move your arm away as quickly as possible. This is an example of a reflex action.

POWER HOUSE

You only have to look at an athlete's body to realize that muscles develop according to the work they have to do. Regular exercise can make muscles stronger and better able to work well. Your heart itself is made of muscle, and a good exercise routine will help it to be more efficient.

ON REFLECTION

In these circumstances, you don't make a conscious decision to move – your nervous system knows there isn't time. You just do it without thinking. The situation registers in your brain a fraction of a second later.

Sudden strenuous effort can take its toll on muscles. This is why it's important to warm up gradually before you exercise. Otherwise you can actually damage your muscles.

FOOD FOR THOUGHT

Do you realize that some of the cereal you ate this morning might at this very moment be being used to make new bone cells? Incredible isn't it? Yet every process carried out by your body requires certain nutrients and energy, and you get these from food. Of course, your body can't use the food in the form that you eat it. That's why your body comes with its own special conversion unit, the digestive system.

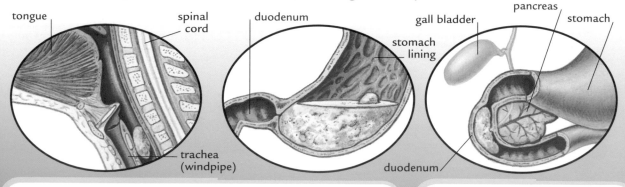

tongue | spinal cord | duodenum | stomach lining | gall bladder | pancreas | stomach | trachea (windpipe) | duodenum

COME ON DOWN!

When you take in food, your teeth break it down into smaller pieces and saliva mixes with it to make it softer. After you swallow, muscles in your throat force the food down into the stomach. (There is a special muscle at the back of your throat that closes your windpipe when you swallow to stop food going down the wrong way and into your lungs.) The lining of your stomach produces acid and special juices called enzymes that break the food down further. Once it has formed a creamy liquid, it is slowly released into the small intestine.

MOVE ALONG THERE!

The small intestine is a narrow tube that twists and turns again and again. The food passes slowly through and mixes with bile from the liver and other juices produced by the pancreas, which digest the food into a form the body can use.

Some of the food you eat could take almost half a century to dissolve in water. The enzymes in your stomach complete the process in a matter of hours.

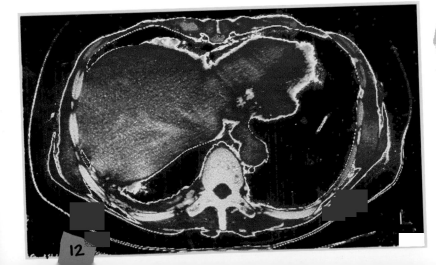

◀ *This computer scan shows the abdomen and a healthy liver.*

WHAT'S ON THE MENU?

Are you ready to order?

I'm not sure. I want something rich in proteins, which are essential for growth and repair of body tissues, and carbohydrates, the body's most immediate source of energy.

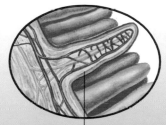

villus (blood vessel for absorption of nutrients)

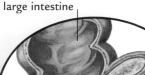

large intestine

appendix

I'd like something with not too many fats. They're important for building cells and insulating the body, but my body can make most of the fats it needs from the rest of the food I eat. It stores any extra fat. Vitamins, though I'll take. Vitamin A can help strengthen the immune system, you know.

TAKING IT ALL IN

The small intestine is lined with thousands of tiny projections called villi, which have very thin walls through which digested food and nutrients – the substances the body needs to promote growth, maintenance, and repair – can pass. These then enter the bloodstream and are taken to the liver.

OVER AND OUT

The food that cannot be digested passes along the small intestine and enters the large intestine. Here some of the water is absorbed, and the rest eventually passes out of the body through the anus as solid waste.

What do you have with minerals? They're vital for various body processes. Something high in fiber too, perhaps. It helps digestion by binding the waste products together in the large intestine.

TIME & MOTION

How long food remains in your system depends on what you have eaten, and when. An apple might pass through your stomach in less than an hour. A large meal could take up to four hours to be broken down.

CONSUMING INTERESTS

Your organs need a healthy balance of different nutrients, but they can't get them on their own. They rely on the food you eat supplying them. A good diet ensures your body receives enough of each food group, but not too much of any one kind.

Some of the things people eat and drink are of little use to the body. Alcohol, for instance, contains plenty of calories, a source of energy, but nothing that the body <u>needs</u>! It's up to you to decide what you put into your stomach!

What did you eat and drink today? Did you enjoy it? Do you think your body "enjoyed" it?

13

SPECIAL DELIVERIES

f you had a present for someone who lived miles away, you would probably rely on a delivery service to get it there. To make sure your body receives everything it needs, you have your own transport system inside you – and it's a 24-hour service! Blood is like a liquid vehicle, carrying all the oxygen and nutrients your body needs to be able to function and taking away any waste products the cells can't use.

LOOP THE LOOP

The blood system is called the circulatory system, because, although it is very complex, it can be thought of as a loop. It consists of the heart and a network of 60,000 miles of blood vessels.

CHAMBER ORGAN

The heart is known the world over as a romantic symbol. In fact it has a much more down-to-earth role. A muscular organ about the size of a fist, it has four chambers – one atrium and one ventricle on each side. Each atrium receives blood from the veins; the ventricles pump the blood to the lungs and around the body.

Your body works hard to remove waste products from your blood system. Even so, some may travel around the body several times before being disposed of.

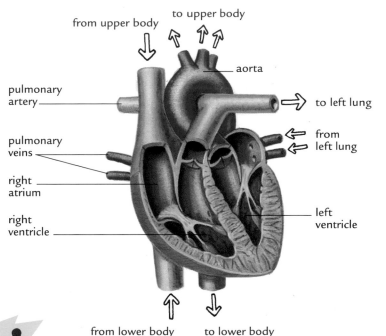

from upper body — to upper body
aorta
pulmonary artery
pulmonary veins
right atrium
right ventricle
to left lung
from left lung
left ventricle
from lower body — to lower body

The heart can't absorb oxygen from the blood passing through it because it goes through too quickly and is under too much pressure. Instead it has its own set of arteries. They're called "coronary arteries" meaning "like a crown," because of the shape they make around the outside of the heart.

HEART TO HEART

Blood travels twice through the heart on its way around the body. It is pumped out once to pick up oxygen from the lungs, then is sent back to the heart to be pumped out again to deliver that oxygen and the rest of the blood's "cargo" to the rest of the body.

BRANCHING OUT

Arteries carry blood from the heart to the lungs and the rest of the body. Veins carry blood back to the heart from the rest of the body. Both divide into smaller and smaller branches, eventually becoming tiny blood vessels called capillaries. Capillaries release the nutrients and oxygen in the blood into the tissues of the body. At the same time carbon dioxide and waste matter from the tissues pass into the blood in the capillaries to be taken by the veins to be disposed of.

Did you know that smoking marijuana, a drug grown from the hemp plant, makes the heart beat faster? This isn't good for the body over a long period of time.

IT'S IN YOUR BLOOD

Blood is composed of red and white cells, floating in a liquid called plasma. Red cells pick up oxygen and release it into the tissues where it is needed. White cells form a major part of the body's defense system against infection. There is one white cell for every 600 red ones; except when your body is fighting off an infection, when the white cells increase.

UNWANTED GIFTS

Your blood is a superbly efficient transportation system, but it isn't choosy about what it carries. Whatever can be absorbed by your body will be, and it will enter your bloodstream and be delivered to all the different organs. For example, chemicals from any drugs – whether smoked, inhaled, or swallowed – will be absorbed by the body and so will cause some physical effect. What the effects are, depends on the drug taken.

How many times have you opened a present and been surprised to discover that it's exactly what you don't want? Unlike you, your organs can't just smile sweetly and pretend everything's fine!

THE BEAT GOES ON...

If someone asked you to bang a drum seventy times in one minute, you probably wouldn't think it too difficult. But how would you feel if you were asked to do the same thing – without stopping or resting – for an hour, or all day long? Or all year? How about for the rest of your life?

70 beats per minute. 60 minutes per hour. 24 hours per day. 365 days per year. 70 x 60 x 24 x 365 = 36,792,000 beats. That's just for one year. Over 70 years, that would be 2,575,440,000 beats!! That's a lot of work!

It certainly is a lot of work, but it's a job that the average person's heart will do during his or her lifetime.

Red and white cells and platelets (in blue), which help blood to clot.

PROTECT AND SERVE

First the bad news: amazing as your body is, it can be damaged by injury or disease. The good news, however, is that your body is equipped with another highly sophisticated system, whose job it is to defend you against any threat to your health and your body's homeostasis. This system is called the immune system.

SPACE INVADERS

Viruses are tiny organisms that can multiply only within another living cell. Once inside they cause the cell to make many new viruses which go on to infect surrounding cells. Diseases caused by viruses include colds, flu, measles, and AIDS.

Bacteria are single-celled organisms. Not all are harmful; some live happily on or within your body. They can, however, cause disease if they get out of hand. For instance, bacteria are responsible for food poisoning and pneumonia.

Smokers of cigarettes or other drugs clog up their breathing passages with tar. This reduces the effectiveness of the hairs, or cilia, in catching any intruding foreign particles — and so handicaps one of the body's natural defenses against germs.

DEFENSE TACTICS

An infection occurs when a virus or disease-causing organism enters your body and your body reacts to handle the invasion.

White cells play the biggest part in controlling and attacking infection. There are three main types – T-cells, B-cells, and NK-Cells.

NK-cells are Natural Killer cells. They can change shape and surround invading substances, taking them apart, and digesting them. B-cells produce substances called antibodies, which lock on to the invading bacteria or virus and prevent them from working on healthy cells. T-cells also attack foreign substances within the body. They are very important because they encourage the NK-cells and B-cells to work faster.

PRODUCTION MANAGER

Some white cells are made in the bone marrow. Others are produced by the lymphatic system. This consists of a network of tubes similar to the blood vessels, although there are far fewer of them. White cells are made in lymph nodes, small swellings at certain points within the lymphatic system. Bacteria that are not destroyed by the white cells in the bloodstream and tissues will be carried to the lymph nodes where white cells will destroy them.

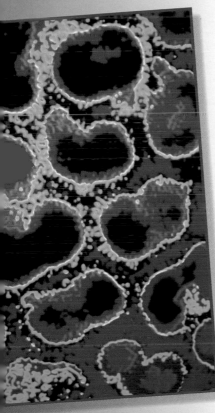

The flu virus (above) is spread through couging and sneezing.

BEEN THERE, DONE THAT!

The B-cells in your body can produce hundreds of antibodies. They need to because each antibody only works on the specific type of bacteria or virus that is causing the problem. The amazing thing is that once your body has produced a particular antibody, it will remain in the bloodstream for a while and the body will remember how to reproduce it quickly if the same invader should attack in the future. This is why a person who has had chickenpox is unlikely to get the same disease again.

> I don't get it. If my body's producing all these antibodies, how come I got the same cold last year?

> That's just it; you didn't. Your body's immune to a cold once you've had it. Unfortunately, there are hundreds of different cold viruses out there.

KEEP OUT!

Skin is more than the carrier bag in which the rest of your body is packed! It is your body's first level of defense against infection. To infect you, an invading organism must find its way through.

HAIR RAISING

Your eyelashes protect your eyes by flicking away dust. Your breathing passages are also lined with tiny, fine hairs, called cilia. These produce a sticky mucus, which traps many foreign particles when you breathe in. You get rid of them when you blow your nose or cough.

HELP YOURSELF

Remember that you don't always have to rely on your body to look after itself. There is a lot that you can do to help it, by being careful about what substances you take into your body, and by not putting yourself at risk of injury or disease in the first place. Emotional safety is as important as being physically fit. Feeling stress and having low self-esteem can have a real effect on your health and can lower your body's ability to fight off disease.

19

KEEPING YOUR BALANCE

Have you ever noticed how some people eat everything in sight and don't seem to put on any weight, while others seem to eat hardly anything and pile on the pounds? This is because people convert and store food in different ways. The process by which food is changed by the body into energy and body tissue is called metabolism. This process is controlled by different organs of the body, and by special substances, hormones, produced by your endocrine system.

SORTING OFFICE

All the blood from the blood vessels in the alimentary canal passes through the liver. The liver is one of the most important organs in maintaining the homeostasis of the body. It has over 500 jobs to do, including:

● Regulating the amount of sugar in your blood. Sugar needs to be present for the cells to produce energy, but too much or too little can have serious health effects.

● Producing bile that helps to dissolve fats, making them easier to absorb and digest.

● Making harmless any poisonous substances that pass into the bloodstream during digestion.

● Storing vitamins, such as vitamins A and D, that are used by the body.

Around 200 billion red cells die and are replaced every day! The dead cells are broken down by the liver. All the chemical processes going on in the liver give off heat as a by-product. So as well as doing everything else, your liver actually contributes to keeping you at the right temperature.

To test how much sugar is in the blood, people with diabetes do a blood glucose test.

To establish the amount of sugar in the blood, a drop of blood is placed on a chemically coated strip, which is then inserted into a digital glucometer. This activates the digital display of the glucose sensor.

TAKE IT AWAY!

The kidneys are two oval-shaped organs that also regulate homeostasis. Their job is also to filter waste products and excess water out of the blood to prevent it from becoming diluted. They do this by absorbing fluid from the capillaries that pass into the kidneys. This fluid passes through a series of tiny tubes, which put back into the blood anything that shouldn't have been removed, and sends the rest on to your bladder, as the waste product, urine. You get rid of this when you go to the bathroom.

BREAKDOWN VEHICLE

The liver has to break down anything the body can't use, or which might harm it, into harmless substances that can be excreted. Alcohol gives the liver extra work to do because it is broken down slowly, flowing around the body for a long time before the liver can complete its work. High alcohol consumption over a long period will seriously harm the liver and other organs in the body, such as the pancreas.

When different hormones in the body have finished their tasks, they are broken down by the liver and the kidneys get rid of them in urine.

CONTROL CENTERS

At certain points in your body are glands that form the endocrine system. These glands produce chemicals called hormones, which travel in the bloodstream and speed up, slow down, or control the processes going on in other organs. Some of the most important glands in your body are:

- The pituitary gland: this produces many hormones. It is the "master" gland controlling many of the other glands and the hormones that they secrete, or release. One of the pituitary hormones controls the operation of the kidneys; another regulates the growth rate of the body.

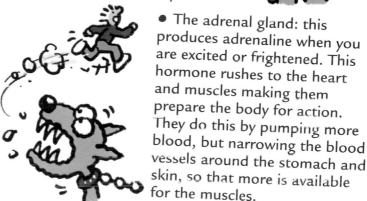

- The adrenal gland: this produces adrenaline when you are excited or frightened. This hormone rushes to the heart and muscles making them prepare the body for action. They do this by pumping more blood, but narrowing the blood vessels around the stomach and skin, so that more is available for the muscles.

- The thyroid gland: this produces a hormone called thyroxine. This affects the rate at which energy is produced in the cells. Too little of it can mean a person is sluggish and may put on a lot of weight.

- The pancreas: this produces a very important hormone called insulin. This controls the level of glucose in the blood and regulates the work of the liver in storing sugar. People with diabetes produce too little insulin and their blood sugar level is too high.

A BUNDLE OF NERVES

If you are part of a group, engaged in carrying out a task, you would have to communicate with other members of the group and they with you, in order to complete the task successfully. To make sure that all your body systems can work well together, you have a communication network inside you. It's called the central nervous system, and consists of your brain, your spinal cord, and the nerves themselves.

WALKIE-TALKIE

Nerve cells, called neurons, pass messages to and from the brain to all parts of the body. These messages are known as impulses, and are actually tiny electrical charges which travel very quickly. They tell all parts of your body exactly what to do and when. So every time you walk, sneeze, breathe, write, chew, and so on, it happens thanks to the communication between the nerves and your brain.

A nerve impulse can travel as fast as 325 feet a second, which is why we can react very quickly when we need to.

A nerve cell is composed of a cell body, which contains the nucleus, and a long nerve "fiber."

MAKING SENSE OF IT ALL

Your five senses – sight, hearing, smell, taste, and touch – all work due to your central nervous system. Light falling on the back of the eye forms an image and sets off impulses in the optic nerve. Air vibrations resonate inside the ear drum and are picked up by nerves in the inner ear. The lining of your nose has groups of sensory cells that pick up chemicals in the air. Your tongue has groups of similar cells, called taste buds, that pick up chemicals in food. And all over your body are thousands of sensory receptors picking up sensations of pressure, cold, heat, and pain, which are all interpreted by the brain.

NO ADDED FLAVORS

Did you know that your sense of smell is 10,000 times more acute than your sense of taste? Your tongue only knows four tastes – sweet, sour, salt, and bitter. Your nose can distinguish many more different chemicals. Your brain registers the flavor of food from a combination of the action of your taste buds and the smell of the food chemicals hitting nasal sensors at the back of your throat.

This doesn't taste right.

Sally's right. There's something odd about it.

I made it the way I always do. I thought it was your favorite.

We've all got blocked noses, that's all. That's why we're not tasting the food the way we normally do.

JUMPIN' JACK FLASH!

Most nerve impulses don't run along just one nerve fiber on their way to the brain. They may need to travel across two or three neurons on their journey. The place at which an impulse transfers from one cell to another is called a "synapse." At a synapse, the end of one nerve fiber is in close contact with another neuron. When an impulse reaches the synapse, it "jumps" across a tiny gap and sets off an impulse in the neighboring cell.

OUCH!

Pain is there for a reason – to stop you from doing whatever is causing the problem! Have you heard the expression "no pain, no gain" to describe exercise? While some forms of exercise may cause some mild discomfort as muscles are worked hard, if you experience any actual pain, you should stop exercising immediately. Far from being good for you, you might in fact be doing yourself harm.

Did you know that nicotine and other drugs affect the nerve impulse's ability to make the jump across a synapse, which is why they can affect your coordination? The messages just don't get through properly.

HEADQUARTERS

The nerves are the cable network in the body, but they need a main switchboard. You have one, of course – it's your brain – and it is responsible for controlling and monitoring everything else that is going on within your body. It is an incredibly complex organ. In fact, scientists have been studying the brain for years and they still only understand a fraction of exactly how it works.

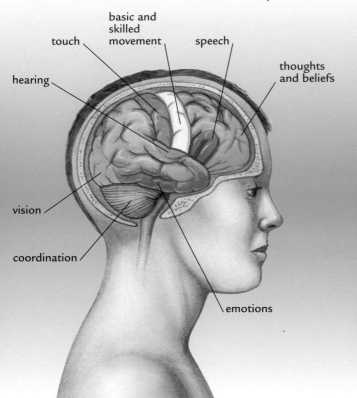

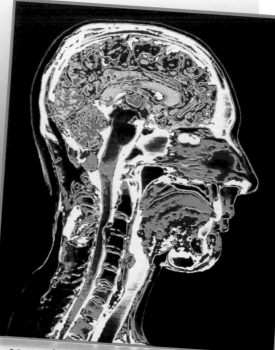

A scan showing the brain and airways.

CONTROL PANEL

Your brain has two distinct halves, which control different functions of the body. The right side of your brain controls the left side of your body and vice versa. The parts of the brain include the medulla, which regulates the heartbeat, breathing, and temperature; the cerebellum, which controls balance and movement; the mid-brain, which handles some reflexes; and the cerebrum, the largest part of the brain, which is concerned with memory, intelligence, and learning ability, and is sometimes known as the gray matter. The cerebral hemispheres (in the cerebrum) contain hundreds of thousands of nerves that allow impulses to travel between different nerve cells.

Your brain comprises approximately 97% of your entire central nervous system – so you'd better take care of it!

MIXED MESSAGES

The brain sends and receives messages by sending impulses along the spinal cord, which in turn cause a certain movement or action to happen in the body. Don't forget, though, that there are hundreds of these impulses being sent out and received all the time. Your brain is so incredibly smart that it can keep track of all the things going on in the body, and still leave you room to think and learn.

Nicotine from tobacco travels quickly to the brain. It causes the brain to speed up the heart rate and increase blood pressure unnecessarily. This can be interpreted as the "buzz" some people say they get from smoking, but it can be very dangerous as it interferes with the body's natural functions.

NOTIONS AND EMOTIONS

Feelings – such as love, hate, happiness, anger, and fear – are powerful influences on people's lives. But where do they come from? In truth, nobody knows exactly, but all feelings can be shown to have specific effects on the body. Whether these effects are caused by the emotion, or whether the emotion leads to the effects, is the cause of some discussion! Emotions also depend on our experiences and how we learn to interpret situations.

I can't go on stage. I'm petrified. My stomach's churning and my hands are sweating.

That's just your body reacting to the fact that you're nervous. You'll be okay.

I'm not nervous at all. I can't wait to get out there. I'm so excited my skin's tingling.

Cocaine – a drug that comes from coca leaves – is known to affect the user's behavior (as many drugs do) as well as have harmful physical side effects. It can alter moods and emotions, leading to feelings of paranoia and depression.

PARTNERSHIP PROJECT

Most people think of themselves as having two parts – their mind and their body. In fact the two are interconnected. The activity within the brain is not only responsible for all the physical functions of the body; it also allows you to think, feel, and imagine.

INTELLIGENCE AGENT

The brain isn't a muscle, but it can still benefit from being exercised. Intelligence is difficult to measure. Most people are good at certain things and less good at others. Learning can be hard work sometimes, but the advantages it offers are worth it. It helps if you find out your strengths and weaknesses. When do you work best? What subjects do you particularly like? If you have problems remembering facts, there are tricks you can learn to make this easier. Learning can be fun. Even things that seem to have no relevance to your life right now can become tremendously important later on.

25

THE TIME OF YOUR LIFE

When you look at a photograph of yourself as a young child, it can be difficult to imagine that the small person staring back at you is you. It seems impossible that you were once half the size you are now, that at one time you needed help dressing or that you could have liked the kinds of things you did when you were five years old. Change is a natural part of life. Over the years, you have undergone many changes, and there are more exciting ones to come!

ALL CHANGE!

IN BOYS:

● *Hair will begin to grow on different parts of the body, such as under the arms, on the face and around the pubic area.*

● *The testes will produce sperm for the first time.*

● *The voice will usually "break" and become deeper.*

● *The penis and testicles will grow larger.*

IN GIRLS:

● *Hair will begin to grow on different parts of the body, such as under the arms and around the pubic area.*

● *Ovulation – the release of an egg by the ovaries – will begin, and girls will start to have periods.*

● *The hips will usually become broader.*

● *The breasts will develop.*

Puberty is a very special period in your life. During puberty, several significant changes occur that alter the body from one of a child to one of a young adult. The age at which puberty happens varies widely, though it's usually around the ages of 10–14.

Once it has begun, boys and girls become physically capable of reproducing – making babies. This is because another body system – the reproductive system – is activated. Above are some of the changes which happen during puberty. It's important for everyone to understand exactly what's in store. By finding out, you can be prepared.

WHOSE BODY IS IT ANYWAY?

Many of the changes you undergo will be completely new. You might feel at times as though your body isn't your own. There will be parts growing, new parts appearing, unfamiliar thoughts and emotions, and an awful lot to think about! Remember that although your body seems to be out of control, it isn't really. It's just in a bit of a rush.

Not since you were a few months old has your body undergone as many changes, all at the same time, as it will during the years of puberty.

Some people experience growth spurts during puberty, and may grow several inches taller in a relatively short period of time. Drugs such as nicotine in tobacco can actually restrict the growth hormones in the body — and so prevent the body from developing normally.

I don't mind everything else, but I wish my voice would change. It's not easy to be taken seriously when you sound like a deflating balloon.

GENERATION GASP!

You aren't the only one trying to become accustomed to the changes going on in your life. Just pity your poor parents. They're trying to keep up too. They might sometimes still treat you as they did when you were younger. They have had a long time to get used to you growing and changing at a reasonable pace, then suddenly – whoosh! Often it can be difficult for them to accept that you are becoming a person in your own right. Adjusting to the "new you" can take time.

THE REST IS UP TO YOU

As you grow older, you will be making choices about your life. To make healthy decisions, you need to know how your body works, and what you can do to make sure it keeps on working properly. You also have to realize that your body is worth caring for. Remember, you can't exist without it, and it can't exist without you!

CHAIN REACTION

You should have worked out by now how interconnected the body systems are: you can't stand without your skeleton, which can't move without your muscles, which couldn't work without energy from digested food, which can't be used without oxygen from your lungs, which would go nowhere without your circulation, which happens because your heart beats, which happens because of nerve impulses, whose messages wouldn't get through unless the brain was there to interpret them, and so on.

ALL FOR ONE AND ONE FOR ALL

The main thing your body relies on to work successfully is YOU. The decisions you make about what you take into your body, how much exercise you do and the day-to-day demands you put on your body can all have an effect on how efficiently your body works.

Hi, I'm Sharon. This is my sister, Fiona. We're identical twins. We're the same height and size, and we lead similar lifestyles. I've found out that my sister's up to four times as likely to have a sudden heart attack as I am, all because she's chosen to do something I've decided not to.

Fiona smokes. She regularly speeds up her heart rate, raises her blood pressure, and deprives her blood of oxygen, all because she smokes. Some decisions can have far-reaching consequences as well as immediate effects.

BALANCING FACTS

Your choices can be influenced by many factors. They may depend on who you listen to, the way you have been brought up, your likes and dislikes, and your view of yourself as a person. As you grow up, you will decide, for instance, what you like to eat and drink, which people you spend time with, whether or not you smoke, or how you will react if someone offers you drugs. Making the right decisions is often a question of weighing the issues for and against a situation, and to do this, it is vital to have all the information you need.

RECIPE FOR HEALTH

Remember, your body has to deal with everything you put inside it. It's important to make sure that you eat enough of the right things to allow your body to be able to carry out its day-to-day functions. This doesn't mean you can never eat hamburgers and fries again, or that you have to give up your favorite chocolate cake. It just means making sure that they're not your whole diet.

Finding out what nutrients are in the food you eat will help to check how your body is likely to react. Keeping a food diary might be a good way to understand your eating habits and decide whether you need to make any changes.

As you get older, there are lots of choices to make about how you are going to spend your time and whom you're going to spend your time with.

ONE IN A MILLION

You're a unique individual – the decisions you make for your body are up to you. You've learned how your body works and why all the various parts are arranged as they are. You can see that your body depends on balance and how you can help it to maintain this. Everyone likes to have a good time, but this doesn't mean taking risks or doing things that you know will harm you or someone else. Being responsible doesn't mean that you can't have fun. Enjoy yourself!

LETTER FROM LIFE EDUCATION

Dear Friends:

The first Life Education Center was opened in Sydney, Australia, in 1979. Founded by the Rev. Ted Noffs, the Life Education program came about as a result of his many years of work with drug addicts and their families. Noffs realized that preventive education, beginning with children from the earliest possible age all the way into their teenage years, was the only long-term solution to drug abuse and other related social problems.

Life Education pioneered the use of technology in a "Classroom of the 21st Century," designed to show how drugs, including nicotine and alcohol, can destroy the delicate balance of human life. In every Life Education classroom, electronic displays show the major body systems, including the respiratory, nervous, digestive and immune systems. There is also a talking brain, a wondrous star ceiling, and Harold the Giraffe, Life Education's official mascot. Programs start in preschool and continue through high school.

Life Education also conducts parents' programs including violence prevention classes, and it has also begun to create interactive software for home and school computers.

There are Life Education Centers operating in seven countries (Thailand, the United States, the United Kingdom, New Zealand, Australia, Hong Kong, and New Guinea), and there is a Life Education home page on the Internet (the address is http://www.lec.org/).

If you would like to learn more about Life Education International contact us at one of the addresses listed below or, if you have a computer with a modem, you can write to Harold the Giraffe at Harold@lec.org and you'll find out that a giraffe can send E-mail!

Let's learn to live.

All of us at the Life Education Center.

Life Education, USA	Life Education, UK	Life Education, Australia	Life Education, New Zealand
149 Addison Ave	20 Long Lane	PO Box 1671	126 The Terrace
Elmhurst, Illinois	London	Potts Point	PO Box 10-769
60126	EC1A 9HL	NSW 2011	Wellington
Tel: 630 530 8999	United Kingdom	Australia	New Zealand
Fax: 630 530 7241	Tel: 0171 600 6969	Tel: 0061 2 358 2466	Tel: 0064 4 472 9620
	Fax: 0171 600 6979	Fax: 0061 2 357 2569	Fax: 0064 4 472 9609

Antibodies Produced by white B-cells in the blood to fight harmful bacteria in the body.

Arteries Blood vessels that carry blood enriched with oxygen from the heart to the body. The exception is the pulmonary artery that takes blood from the heart to the lungs for a new supply of oxygen.

Atria The smallest of the heart's four cavities or chambers. The two atria pump blood down to the two larger ventricles.

Bacteria Small single-celled organisms, some of which can cause illness if they get into the body.

Capillaries The smallest of the three types of blood vessels. Capillaries connect the ends of the arteries with the ends of the veins.

Carbohydrates Energy-giving substances found in foods containing starch and sugar, such as bread, potatoes, pasta, cakes, and cookies.

Chromosomes Thread-like structures, usually found in a cell's nucleus, that contain genes.

DNA Deoxyribonucleic acid, the substance found in chromosomes that carries genes.

Genes Made up of DNA and forming part of a chromosome, genes determine an individual's characteristics, such as sex, height, eye, and hair color.

Hormones Chemical substances produced by glands and carried in the blood to the part of the body where they are needed.

Ligaments The strong tissues linking bones together to form joints.

Minerals Like vitamins, essential for good health but only required in minute amounts.

Nicotine A chemical in tobacco, which is addictive.

Protein Vital part of a diet, necessary for growth, repair of damaged cells, and general health.

Synapse The minute gap between two neurons (nerve cells) where the nerve impulse is passed on by a chemical messenger.

Veins Blood vessels that take blood – from which the oxygen has been absorbed by the body tissues – back to the heart. The exception is the pulmonary vein that takes blood enriched with oxygen from the lungs back to the heart.

Ventricles The largest of the heart's four chambers. The right ventricle pumps blood to the lungs and the left, the larger of the two, pumps blood to the rest of the body.

Viruses Tiny organisms that can only live and multiply inside other living cells. Viruses cause diseases such as colds, measles, and AIDS.

Vitamins Nutrients essential for the body's health, but only needed in very small quantities.

FURTHER INFORMATION

The following organizations are useful sources of further information about topics covered in this book.

American Heart Association
7272 Greenville Avenue
Dallas, TX 75321
Telephone: 214-373-6300
Toll-free: 800-242-8721
Fax: 214-706-1341

President's Council on Physical Fitness and Sports
701 Pennsylvania Ave., NW
Suite 250
Washington, DC 20004
Telephone: 202-272-3421
Fax: 202-504-2064

TARGET
Helping Students Cope with Tobacco, Alcohol, and Other Drugs
11724 NW Plaza Circle
PO Box 20626
Kansas City, MO 64195
Telephone: 816-464-5400
Toll-free: 800-366-6667
Fax: 816-464-5571

INDEX